YORKSHIRE
COUNTRY RECIPES

COMPILED BY
MOLLY PERHAM

Maidstone

YORKSHIRE

The large county of Yorkshire is a mixture of rich and varied countryside - the gentle green Dales, the spectacular limestone regions, the rugged moors - and of large cities born during the Industrial Revolution. Traditional dishes vary between town and country areas - country housewives have had access to excellent, fresh farm produce, whereas in the towns dishes evolved that could be left to cook on the hob while the family were out at work all day. The one thing the dishes have in common is that they are substantial and economical, to satisfy the hearty appetites of both farmers and mill workers.

The best-known Yorkshire specialty, the Yorkshire Pudding, is a prime example of a cheap and filling dish. Eaten at the beginning of a meal, it took the edge off the appetite, to eke out the meat when money was scarce. This, and other savoury puddings, still form a major part of the Yorkshireman's diet..

Good filling meals were an essential ingredient of country life: they were not only a means of sustaining energy in a hard climate, they also provided a chance to meet friends and neighbours.For centuries oats were staple food of the hilly areas. Each village had a kiln in which the grain was parched before being ground, and this became a meeting place where the local people gathered to exchange gossip and discuss the affairs of the day. The ground oatmeal was stored in a wooden ark in the home, pressed down firmly. The oatmeal was made into bread, cakes and the hasty pudding – from which many varieties of savoury and sweet puddings developed.

Mutton, pork, ham, bacon, poultry and game have always formed an important part of the farmhouse diet - but with roast taking pride of place. The coastline is short, so most of the fish comes from the port of Hull - haddock being the most popular choice for local fish and chips.

The cheese of the Yorkshire Dales is Wensleydale. A

Yorkshireman will eat it with almost everything, including fruit cake and apple pie. White Wensleydale, which is the most common, is soft and flaky with a velvety texture. Blue Wensleydale is rich and creamy and veined with blue.

The recipe for Wensleydale cheese came from the Cistercian monks, who settled in the Dales at Jervaulx in early Norman times. They made it with ewe's milk, and it was rather like Roquefort cheese, made in that part of southern France from which the monks originally came. When the monasteries were dissolved cheese making was continued by the farmers' wives, but since the 17th century cow's milk has been used. These days Wensleydale is not produced on the farms but in enormous creameries such as the one at Gayle near Hawes. Small amounts of Cotherstone cheese are still made on some farms in the Dales. This has a soft texture and a rich flavour, and is well worth trying.

Monks were also responsible for another Yorkshire speciality - the Black Friars introduced liquorice extract for use in medicines, and in the 18th century treacle, sugar and flour were added to produce Pontefract Cakes. Treacle is used in many traditional Yorkshire foods, such as treacle tart, gingerbread, parkin and toffee - and even in salad dressing.

There has always been a close connection in Yorkshire between food and religious festivals, each having its own traditional dishes. Christmas Eve supper consisted of frumenty, spice cake, mince pies and cheese. On Christmas Day a plum pudding would follow the roast. Large goose pies were traditionaly made on the feast of St. Stephen, December 26th, some being distributed to needy neighbours, and one kept for Candlemas on February 2nd. Christmas Pies were also made and sent to London as presents. At Shrovetide pancakes were served on the Tuesday, followed by apple fritters on the

Wednesday. Fish pie was traditional on Good Friday, and curd tarts on Whitsuntide. Saints' days were remembered with special food too - Cattern Cakes on St. Catherine's Day, and Wilfra Tarts were to commemorate St. Wilfred. Tradition, too, marked the important events of a person's life - in the 18th century cakes were reserved for special occasions such as christenings, engagements and weddings.

Perhaps because of the climate tea has always been a sit-down meal with filling pies, buns and cakes. Walkers coming off the fells and dales will find the Yorkshire fare as substantial and satisfying as the hospitality for which the county is renowned.

'An apple pie without Wensleydale cheese
is like a kiss without a squeeze.'

Anon - Traditional

RECIPES

FESTIVALS and SPECIAL OCCASIONS

YORKSHIRE PUDDING

Serves 8

Traditionally a savoury pudding was served with gravy before the meat to take the edge off the appetite. In large hungry families the saying was "Them as has most pudding can have most meat"

Yorkshire Pudding was baked in a dripping pan underneath the beef as it roasted above the fire. As the juices dripped from the joint they were absorbed into the pudding. This can be done in the oven if the beef is put on a stand or grid in a roasting tray, and the batter is poured in about 20 minutes before the beef is ready. Every Yorkshire family has its own method of making this traditional dish - but however it is made, it should be about 1/2 inch (1 cm) thick, light and crisp at the edges. It is best to prepare the batter when you put the beef in the oven, as it improves if left to stand.

6 oz (175 g) plain flour
A pinch of salt
2 eggs
1 pint (600 ml/2 1/2 cups) milk

Sift the flour and salt into a mixing basin and make a well in the centre. Break the eggs into the well and draw in some of the flour from the sides.

Gradually add the milk, beating well between each addition, until the batter is smooth and free from lumps

Allow the batter to stand for at least 1 hour.

Half an hour before the joint of beef will be ready put a little dripping from the roast into a baking tin.

Preheat the tin in the oven until the fat is smoking.

Pour in the batter. Bake for 20-25 minutes at the top of the oven until the pudding is crisp at the edges and golden brown.

Serve the Yorkshire Pudding with thick gravy made from the meat juices, or with onion gravy.

Oven: 400°F/200°C Gas Mark 6

ONION GRAVY

3 tablespoons of dripping from the joint
2 onions
2 oz (50 g) plain flour
1 pint (600 ml/2½ cups) stock from cooking the vegetables
2 teaspoons vinegar
Salt and pepper

Peel and slice the onions and cook gently in the dripping for 4-5 minutes until they are soft and transparent.

Sprinkle over the flour, stir, and cook for a further minute.

Gradually add the vegetable stock, stirring well to prevent lumps forming.

Bring to the boil and simmer gently for about 10 minutes.

Add the vinegar, and season to taste.

POTATO AND ONION SOUP

Serves 4

This is a cheap and really filling soup for cold winter days.

1 lb (450 g) potatoes
2 onions
2 carrots
About 1/4 pint (150 ml/2/3 cup milk)
Salt and pepper
Grated cheese

Peel the potatoes and cut into smallish pieces.

Slice the onions and carrots.

Put all the vegetables into a saucepan and barely cover them with water.

Add a pinch of salt.

Bring to the boil and simmer until the vegetables are tender.

Pour off some of the water and add enough milk to make a thick lumpy soup.

Add pepper and grated cheese according to taste.

RASPBERRY VINEGAR

Yorkshire Pudding was often served sprinkled with raspberry vinegar as a first course, or as a dessert. This is a traditional home-made recipe.

4 quarts (4.5 litres) raspberries
1 quart (1.15 litres) white vinegar
3 lbs (1.5 kg) sugar

Put the raspberries into a stone jar (or plastic would do), and pour over the vinegar.

Leave to stand, uncovered, for 4 days, stirring twice a day.

After 4 days cover the jar and leave for another 4 days, stirring once a day.

At the end of this time strain the raspberries through a sieve or muslin bag.

Put the liquid into a preserving pan and add the sugar.

Heat gently until all the sugar has dissolved, then simmer for 10 minutes.

Store the raspberry vinegar in bottles and use as required.

FISH AND CHIPS

Serves 4

In Yorkshire when you order this favourite meal it comes with mushy peas, sliced white bread and butter and a pot of strong tea with milk and sugar. Haddock is the preferred fish, and the chips are thick and cooked in beef dripping.

6 oz (175 g) plain flour
1 teaspoon bicarbonate of soda
A pinch of salt
1/2 pint (300 ml/1 1/4 cups) water
2 lbs (900 g) potatoes
Beef dripping
4 haddock fillets

Sift the flour, bicarbonate of soda and salt into a large mixing basin. Make a well in the centre and gradually pour in the water, drawing in the flour from the sides.

Beat well until you have a smooth batter, free from lumps. Leave to stand for about 1 hour.

Meanwhile peel the potatoes and cut lengthways into thick chips.

Heat the dripping in a pan until it is hazy. To test whether it is hot enough drop in one small chip and see if it sizzles.

Fry the chips until they are crisp and golden, and keep warm in a preheated oven.

Lightly dust the haddock fillets with flour and dip them in the batter.

Deep fry the fish in the same fat in which the chips were cooked, until golden all over.

Serve the fish and chips with salt and vinegar.

If you want to make this dish really traditional, serve mushy peas.

Soak some dried marrowfat peas overnight, then next day boil them until soft and mushy.

SMOKED HADDOCK

Serves 4

1-1$^{1/4}$ lbs (0.5 kg) smoked haddock fillet
1/2 pint (300 ml/1$^{1/4}$ cups) milk
Salt and pepper
8 oz (225 g) tomatoes
4 oz (100 g) button mushrooms
1/2 oz (15 g) butter

Cut the fillet into four portions and place in a buttered ovenproof dish.

Pour over the milk and season to taste.

Skin the tomatoes, chop finely and add to the fish.

Slice the mushrooms and add to the fish.

Dot the top with butter.

Cover the dish with buttered greaseproof paper.

Bake in a moderate oven for 15 minutes.

Oven: 350°F/180°c   Gas Mark 4

HERRINGS WITH MUSTARD SAUCE Serves 4

This sauce used to be served with a boar's head at Christmas time in some Yorkshire pubs. It goes equally well with herring or with pork.

4 fresh herrings
1 oz (25 g) plain flour
A pinch of salt
1/2 pint (300 ml/1 1/4 cups) milk
1 oz (25 g) sugar
1/2 oz (15 g) butter
1 large teaspoon mustard
1 tablespoon vinegar

Wipe and dry the herrings.

Remove the heads and score across the back and sides, but avoid cutting the roe.

Sprinkle with salt and pepper.

Cook under a hot grill for 10-15 minutes, turning once.

To make the sauce:

Put the flour and salt into a basin.

Add enough milk to make a thick paste, then gradually add the rest of the milk, beating well until the mixture is free from lumps.

Put a drop of water into a saucepan and when it boils add the milk mixture.

Stir over a low heat until the mixture thickens.

Add the sugar and butter.

Mix the vinegar with the mustard and add to the sauce.

Pour the sauce over the herrings and serve hot.

CRAYFISH

Serves 4

This freshwater crustacean is seldom found nowadays but it used to be widely found in the inland streams of the Yorkshire Dales, and cooked over an open fire. Crayfish are rather like small lobsters in appearance.

2 dozen crayfish
Lemon juice

Boil the crayfish in salted water for about 15 minutes, until they are bright red.

Rinse them in cold water and remove the shells.

Sprinkle with lemon juice and eat with brown bread and butter.

SALMON WITH CUCUMBER

Serves 4

4 salmon steaks
Salt and pepper
2 oz (50 g) butter
1 tablespoon white wine
Juice of half a lemon
8 oz (225 g) cucumber
A sprig of parsley

Put the steaks in a buttered ovenproof dish and season with salt and pepper.

Cut the butter into small pieces and put them on top of the fish.

Add the wine and half the lemon juice.

Cover with foil and bake in a moderate oven for 20 minutes.

Peel and dice the cucumber and simmer gently in a little water until it is tender.

Drain thoroughly and put onto a serving dish.

Sprinkle over the finely chopped parsley and the remaining lemon juice.

Peel the skins from the baked salmon steaks and arrange them with the cucumber on the serving dish.

Strain the cooking liquid and pour over the top.

Oven: 350°f/180°C Gas Mark 4

LING PIE

Serves 4

Ling are a member of the cod family seldom available these days except on the Yorkshire coast. They can grow much larger than cod - sometimes up to 7 feet (2 metres) long.

1 lb (450 g) ling
1 oz (25 g) plain flour
Salt and pepper
4 oz (100 g) bacon
2 hardboiled eggs
1 small onion
1/2 pint (300 ml/1 1/4 cups) milk
12 oz (350 g) puff pastry

Cut the fish into four portions.

Coat with flour and season with salt and pepper.

Place in buttered ovenproof dish.

Chop the bacon and slice the eggs and onions and add these to the dish.

Pour over the milk.

Roll out the pastry to make a lid.

Brush with milk or beaten egg to glaze.

Bake in a hot oven for 10 minutes, then reduce the temperature and cook for a further 20 minutes, until the pastry is well risen and golden brown.

Oven: 425°F/220°C Gas Mark 7
Reduce to: 350°F/180°C Gas Mark 4

WAKEFIELD RABBIT

Serves 4

1 rabbit
Seasoned flour
1 egg, beaten
2 oz (50 g) dried breadcrumbs
1 level teaspoon mixed dried herbs
Cayenne pepper
Salt
1 oz (25 g) lard

Prepare and joint the rabbit into four portions.

Dust the joints with seasoned flour.

Dip them in the beaten egg.

Mix the breadcrumbs with the herbs, pepper and salt and coat the joints with the mixture.

Put the joints in a roasting tin and dot the top with lard.

Roast in a moderate oven for about 1 1/2 hours, until the joints have a crisp finish.

Oven: 350°F/180°C   Gas Mark 4

ROAST GOOSE AND SAVOURY PUDDING

Serves 8

Like the better known Yorkshire Pudding, this savoury pudding is also served with - or before- roast meat, and is particularly good with goose or duckling. Roast goose is traditionally served at Michaelmas, at the end of September.

1 goose, weighing 8-10 lbs (3.5-4.5 kg)
will take about $2^{1/2}$ hours to roast
Seasoned flour

For the savoury pudding:
1 lb (450 g) stale white bread
6 oz (175 g) shredded suet
3 boiled and chopped onions
2 teaspoons chopped sage
2 teaspoons chopped marjoram
A pinch of grated nutmeg
Salt and pepper
2 eggs

Rub the flour all over the goose breast, thighs and legs.

Place in a roasting tin in a hot oven.

After 30 minutes remove from the oven and prick with a sharp fork all over the breast and thighs, wherever there is a lot of fat.

Reduce the heat to moderate and continue roasting for another 2 hours.

To make the savoury pudding:

Break the bread into a mixing basin and pour on sufficient boiling water to soak it.

Mash with a fork and mix in the shredded suet, chopped onions and herbs.

Season with nutmeg, salt and pepper.

Bind the ingredients together with the eggs.

Put the mixture into a greased baking tin and bake alongside the meat for the last 30 minutes, until crisp and golden brown.

Slice and serve the pudding with the roast goose and thick gravy made from the pan juices.

Oven: 400°F/200°C Gas Mark 6
Reduce to: 350°F/180°C Gas Mark 4

PIGEON PIE

Serves 6

2 pigeons
8 oz (225 g) rump steak
2 rashers of bacon
Salt and pepper
Stock
2 hard-boiled eggs
12 oz (350 g) puff pastry

Cut each pigeon into four pieces. Slice the beef and bacon.

Put all these into a large pie dish in layers, seasoning each layer.

Pour over enough stock to just cover the meat.

Cover the pie dish with foil and bake in a moderate oven for about 1 1/2 hours, until the meat is cooked.

Take out of the oven, remove the foil, and allow to cool.

Slice the hard-boiled eggs and arrange on top of the meat.

Roll out the pastry to a round which is slightly larger than the dish.

Cut a strip from round the edge and use it to line the rim of the dish.

Moisten the strip with water and put on the pastry lid.

Seal and trim the edges and make a hole in the top.

Use any pastry trimmings to decorate the pie.

Brush with milk or beaten egg to glaze.

Increase the heat of the oven and bake the pie for a further 30-40 minutes until the pastry is well-risen and golden brown.

Oven : 350°F/180°C Gas Mark 4
Increase to: 400°F/200°C Gas Mark 6

MUTTON PIES

Makes 12

1 lb (450 g) mutton or lamb
2 onions
1/2 pint (300 ml/1 1/4 cups) water
Salt and pepper
1 oz (25 g) flour
1 tablespoon chopped parsley
12 oz (350 g) shortcrust pastry

Dice the meat and chop the onions finely.

Put them in a pan with the water, and season with salt and pepper.

Bring to the boil, cover, and simmer until the meat is tender.

Blend the flour with a little water, add to the pan and continue simmering until the gravy has thickened.

Leave to cool, then add the chopped parsley.

Roll out the pastry on a floured surface and cut into rounds to line some greased patty tins.

Spoon some filling into each, and cover with a lid.

Prick the top of each pie with a fork, and brush with milk or beaten egg to glaze.

Bake in a moderate oven for about 20 minutes, until golden brown.

Oven : 400°F/200°C Gas Mark 6

YORKSHIREMAN'S GOOSE

Serves 4

This cheap dish - made of ox liver and eaten by the poor - was jokingly called poor man's or Yorkshireman's goose.

1 lb (450 g) ox liver
Seasoned flour
1 oz (35 g) lard
3 onions
1 tablespoon chopped sage
1/2 pint (300 ml/1¼ cups) stock
1 lb (450 g) potatoes
Butter

Slice the liver thinly and coat in the flour.

Melt the lard in a pan and fry the onions until soft.

Add the liver and fry lightly.

Put the liver and onions in an ovenproof dish.

Sprinkle with chopped sage.

Pour over the stock.

Peel, thinly slice the potatoes and arrange these on the top.

Cover with foil and bake in a moderate oven for 1 hour.

Remove the foil for the last 20 minutes of cooking time and brush the potatoes with melted butter so that they are brown.

Oven: 350°F/180°C Gas Mark 4

BEEF SAUSAGES

Makes 6-8

In Yorkshire beef sausages are traditionally made longer and thinner than pork ones.

1 lb (450 g) lean minced beef
8 oz (225 g) beef suet
4 oz (100 g) fresh white breadcrumbs
Salt and pepper
Sausage skins

Mix the beef, suet and breadcrumbs together.

Season with salt and pepper.

Stuff the mixture into the sausage skins, twisting the ends to secure.

Fry until brown and cooked right through.

Serve with Yorkshire Pudding and onion gravy for a really filling meal.

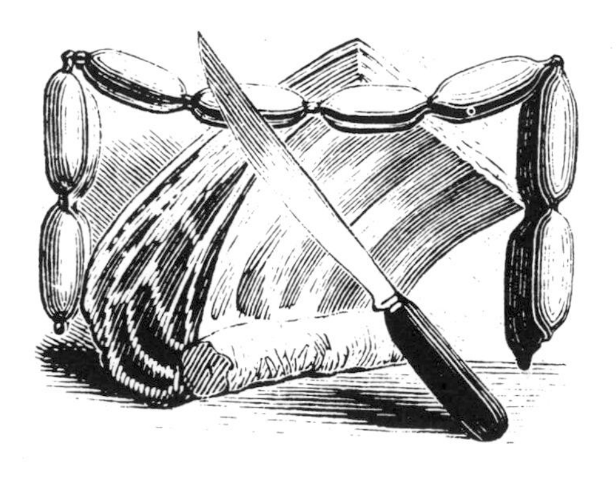

SPICED BEEF

Serves 8-10

Served with salad and pickled onions, this tasty beef is often preferred to ham. It will keep in the refrigerator for a week, or in a freezer for months.

2 lbs (900 g) skirt of beef
Salt
1/2 teaspoon black pepper
1/2 teaspoon ground cloves
1 onion
1 carrot

Rub the beef well with dry salt and leave it overnight.

Next day drain off all the liquid and dry the meat well.

Rub the pepper and cloves into the beef, particularly into the slashes where the bones were removed.

Roll up very tightly and tie with string.

Put into a saucepan with the chopped onion and carrot and cover with water.

Bring to the boil, cover, and simmer gently for, 2-2 1/2 hours until the beef is tender.

Lift out the meat, drain well and reserve the stock.

Remove the string, put the beef under a pastry board with weights on top and leave overnight.

Boil the stock briskly until reduced to a quarter of the original amount.

Pour this over the top of the cold beef to glaze.

MEAT AND POTATO PIE

Serves 4

In East Yorkshire potatoes replace the kidneys in the traditional steak and kidney pie.

1 lb (450 g) stewing steak
Seasoned flour
1 oz (25 g) lard
1 onion
1/2 pint (300 ml/1 1/4 cups) stock
8 oz (225 g) potatoes
8 oz (225 g) shortcrust or puff pastry

Cut the steak into small cubes and toss them in the flour.

Melt the lard in a saucepan and fry the sliced onion and meat until brown.

Cover with stock, bring to the boil and smmer for 1 1/2 hours or until the meat is tender.

Put the meat in a pie dish.

Add the potatoes, cut into dice.

Roll out the pastry to make a lid and make a hole in the top.

Brush the top with beaten egg or milk to glaze.

Bake in a moderately hot oven for 1 hour until the pastry is well-risen and golden brown.

Oven: 400°F/200°C   Gas Mark 6

TRIPE AND ONIONS

Serves 4

2 lbs (900 g) dressed tripe
1 lb (450 g) onions
1/2 pint (300 ml/ 1 1/4 cups) milk
1/2 pint (300 ml/ 1 1/4 cups) water
Salt and pepper
1 oz (25 g) butter
1 oz (25 g) flour
2 oz (50 g) grated cheese

Cut the tripe into bite-sized pieces.

Peel and slice the onions.

Put the tripe and the onions into a saucepan and add the milk and water.

Season with salt and pepper.

Bring to the boil, cover, and simmer for about 1 hour, until the tripe is tender.

Soften the butter and mix it with the flour to form a ball.

Break this into small pieces and add them to the tripe and onions, stirring all the time until the sauce thickens.

Transfer to an ovenproof dish and sprinkle with the cheese.

Bake in a hot oven for 1/2 hour, or put under the grill until the top is golden brown.

Oven: 425°F/220°C   Gas Mark 7

VEAL AND OYSTERS

Serves 4

1 lb (450 g) fillet of veal
8 oysters
Seasoned flour
1 egg
Breadcrumbs
1 oz (25 g) butter

Cut the veal into four portions.

Flatten the meat with a wett rolling pin until it is 1/2 inch (1 cm) thick.

Cut a slit in each piece with the point of a sharp knife.

Remove the oysters from their shells and reserve the liquid.

Stuff two oysters into each piece of veal.

Dust the veal with the flour.

Brush with beaten egg and coat with breadcrumbs.

Melt the butter in a pan and fry the coated veal until the oustide is golden brown and the meat is tender.

Lift out on to a serving dish to keep warm.

Add the oyster liquid to the juices in the pan and stir thoroughly.

Pour over the veal.

Serve garnished with slices of lemon.

RAISED VEAL AND HAM PIE Serves 10-12

Raised pies are part of classic English cooking. Traditionally, the hot water crust pastry is "raised" around the meat filling by hand, an operation that requires great skill. The task is much simpler with a pie mould, which can be bought in traditional shapes. A loose-bottomed cake tin makes an acceptable substitute. The pie crust was called a 'coffyn'.

$1^{1/2}$ lbs (675 g) hot water crust pastry
$1^{1/2}$ lbs (675 g) veal
8 oz (225 g) ham
A sprig of parsley
Salt and pepper
3 hard-boiled eggs
1 egg, beaten, for glazing
1/2 pint (300 ml/$1^{1/4}$ cups) rich stock

For the hot water crust pastry:
1 lb (450 g) plain flour
4 oz (100 g) lard
A pinch of salt
8 fl oz (250 ml/1 cup) water

To make hot water crust pastry

Sift the flour and salt into a warm mixing bowl.

Make a well in the centre, and keep the bowl in a warm place.

Heat the lard and water in a saucepan until boiling.

Pour the melted lard into the flour, drawing in the flour from the sides and mixing with a wooden spoon.

Knead thoroughly.

Reserve a quarter of the pastry for the lid, leaving it in a warm place covered with a cloth. Roll out the remaining pastry into a thick round shape. Work the pastry out from the centre to make a round hollow.

Thin out the sides a little, and press the filling in firmly to support the sides.

Continue working the sides up along the filling, shaping the pie at the same time. This must be done while the pastry is still wam.

When the pie is a good round shape, roll out the lid from the reserved pastry, wet the inner top edges with cold water, put on the lid and press the edges firmly together to seal.

Pin a double thickness of greaseprooof paper round the pie to preserve its shape during baking and to prevent it from becoming too brown.

Put the pie on a baking sheet and bake in a hot oven for the first 30 minutes, then reduce the temperature to moderate and bake for a further 2 hours. Leave to cool.

Pour the warm stock through the hole in the centre of the pie to fill the space inside. Leave until the stock has set to a jelly.

To make the filling:

Cut the veal and ham into dice. Place a layer of veal in the base of the pastry mould and sprinkle with chopped parsley, salt and pepper.

Add a layer of chopped ham, and arrange the hard-boiled eggs in the meat.

Repeat with layers of veal, seasonings and ham until the mould is filled.

Cover the pie with the remaining pastry, making a hole in the lid.

Use any scraps of pastry to decorate the top.

Brush with beaten egg to glaze.

Oven: 425°F/220°C Gas Mark 7
Reduce to: 325°F/160°C Gas Mark 3

RAISED PORK PIE

Serves 10-12

3 lbs (1.5 kg) sparerib of pork
Salt and pepper
1½ lbs (675 g) hot water crust pastry
1 tablespoon chopped sage
1/2 teaspoon grated nutmeg
1 egg
1/4 oz (7 g) gelatine

Make hot water crust pastry (see previous recipe).

Trim the meat from the bones and chop into small dice.

Put the bones in a pan, cover with water and season with salt and pepper.

Bring to the boil and simmer for 2 hours to make stock.

Mix the diced pork with the chopped sage and nutmeg, and season with salt and pepper. Put the mixture into the pastry mould.

Cover the pie with the remaining pastry, making a hole in the lid.

Use any scraps of pastry to decorate the top. Brush the top with beaten egg to glaze.

Put the pie on a baking sheet in a hot oven for the first 30 minutes, then reduce the temperature to moderate and cook for a further 2 hours.

Leave the pie to cool.

Strain the stock, mix with the gelatine dissolved in 1 tablespoon hot water and pour into the pie.

Serve cold.

Oven: 425°F/220°C Gas Mark 7
Reduce to: 325°F/160°C Gas Mark 3

YORK HAM

York hams are large, weighing up to 24 lbs (11 kg), and are rather long in shape because of the way they are cut off the bacon flitch. A flitch is a side of bacon that has had the hind leg removed before curing. York hams are dry salted and lightly smoked, and the original ones are supposed to have got their taste from being smoked in the sawdust left after building York Minster. This is an old Yorkshire recipe for curing a pig.

1 pig
6 lbs (3 kg) salt
8 oz (225 g) saltpetre
1 lb (450 g) sugar

Lay the pig on a cold slab skin side up.

Rub the shoulder and hams well with salt and leave overnight.

Next day cover the slab with plenty of salt and lay the pig on it skin side downwards.

Rub salt well in.

Sprinkle with saltpetre and sugar and leave for 3 - 4 weeks.

Wash well with cold water to remove surplus salt.

Smoke over oak sawdust.

HASLET

Serves 4

In the 19th century, farmers' wives used to bind together the offal of a pig with the caul (the skin that surrounds the suet) to make haslet. These days cauls are not easily obtainable, so the mixture can be put straight into a greased tin.

1 lb (450 g) pig's offal - a mixture of kidney, liver, sweetbreads, heart, etc.
A pig's caul
2 onions
4 oz (100 g) oatmeal
Dried or fresh herbs - sage, thyme and parsley
Salt and pepper
1 oz (25 g) lard

Soak the caul in water for a couple of hours.

Boil the onions until they are soft.

Mince the offal and the onion together.

Add the oatmeal and finely chopped herbs.

Season the mixture with salt and pepper.

Put the mixture into the caul and stitch up tightly.

Place in a roasting tin.

Dot the top with lard.

Bake in a hot oven for 45-50 minutes.

Oven: 425°F/220°C Gas Mark 7

STUFFED LEG OF PORK

Serves 6

3 lbs (1.15 kg) leg of pork, boned
4 oz (100 g) fresh white breadcrumbs
2 oz (50 g) currants
Sage
Ground mace
Salt and pepper

Place the pork in a roasting pan.

Soak the breadcrumbs in water and squeeze until nearly dry.

Mix in the currants.

Season with sage, mace, salt and pepper according to taste.

Use this mixture to stuff the pork.

Roast in a hot oven for 15 minutes, then reduce the temperature and cook for a further 1 1/2 hours.

Oven: 425°F/220°C Gas Mark 7
Reduce to: 350°F/180°C Gas Mark 4

SAUSAGE ROLL

Serves 4

Traditionally this sausage roll would have been tied into a floured pudding cloth and boiled.

8 oz (225 g) lean pork or veal
8 oz (225 g) ham or bacon
8 oz (225 g) fresh white breadcrumbs
A pinch of mace and cayenne pepper
Salt
2 small eggs

Mince the meats finely. Mix with the breadcrumbs.

Season with mace, cayenne pepper and salt.

Bind the mixture together with the beaten eggs.

Turn into a greased pudding basin, cover with greaseproof paper and steam for 3 hours - or reduce the cooking time to 1 hour by using a pressure cooker.

Leave to cool, and serve with salad and pickle.

YORKSHIRE SALAD

Piquant sauces made with vinegar have always been popular in Yorkshire. This salad is often served with roast meats. A spoonful of black treacle is sometimes added.

1 lettuce
1 small onion (or 2-3 spring onions)
A sprig of mint
1 teaspoon sugar
3 tablespoons (1/4 cup) vinegar

Finely shred the lettuce leaves, onions and mint, and put them in a salad bowl.

Dissolve the sugar in the vinegar and pour over the salad.

DOCK PUDDING

Around the Calder Valley area of Yorkshire sweet dock leaves, rather like spinach, are made into a pudding that is fried in bacon fat and eaten for breakfast or high tea. The local people claim it is an excellent spring tonic.

2 lbs (900 g) dock leaves
8 oz (225 g) nettles
2 onions
A handful of oatmeal
Salt and pepper
2 oz (50 g) butter

Thoroughly wash the dock leaves and nettles and remove the stalks.

Peel and finely chop the onions, and cook them in a little water with the dock leaves and nettles until tender.

Add the oatmeal and season to taste with salt and pepper.

Boil for 20 minutes, stirring occasionally.

Strain off any liquid, add the butter and leave to cool.

Fry spoonfuls of the pudding with bacon for breakfast.

If not required immediately, it may be stored in a large jar.

APPLE BATTER WITH GAMMON RASHERS

Serves 4

This is served for high tea in Yorkshire

8 gammon rashers

For the apple batter:
4 oz (100 g) self-raising flour
A pinch of salt
2 oz (50 g) sugar
1/2 pint (300 ml/1 1/4 cups) milk
2 large cooking apples
3 oz (75 g) butter

To make the apple batter:

Sift the flour and salt into a mixing basin.

Add the sugar.

Mix to a smooth batter with the milk.

Peel, core and thinly slice the apples.

Add them to the batter.

Grease a baking tin with some of the butter.

Add the rest of the butter to the batter.

Pour the batter into the tin.

Bake in a hot oven for 20 minutes, then reduce the temperature and bake for a further 20 minutes.

To cook the gammon rashers:

Bake the gammon rashers in the oven at the same time.

Serve the gammon together with the apple pudding.

Oven: 400°F/200°C Gas Mark 6
Reduce to: 350°F/180°C Gas Mark 4

BLOATER PASTE

Serves 4

A bloater is a smoked herring. It is smoked whole and ungutted, not split open down the back like a kipper. It also has a stronger smoked flavour. Fish pastes are served for breakfast or supper on hot buttered toast. They will keep for several weeks in a refrigerator, or may be frozen.

4 bloaters
2 teaspoons lemon juice
About 4 oz (100 g) butter
Pepper
2 hard-boiled eggs

Simmer the bloaters in boiling water for 10-15 minutes until the flesh comes away easily from the bone.

Weigh the flesh and allow half that amount of butter.

Mince the bloater flesh finely.

Add the lemon juice and pepper to taste.

Pound the flesh with the butter to a smooth paste.

Chop the hard-boiled eggs finely and mix into the paste.

Pack the paste into individual dishes.

Pour clarified butter over the top to seal.

BLACK PUDDING

There has always been great rivalry between Yorkshire and Lancashire over which county makes the better black pudding. An international black pudding championship takes place in France each year, and Yorkshire has been amongst the winners several times. The basic ingredient is pig's blood, and the filling mixture is stuffed into intestine skins before the pudding is boiled. However the pudding can just as easily be baked in a greased baking tin.

8 oz (225 g) pork fat
1 onion
4 oz (100 g) pearl barley
4 oz (100 g) fine oatmeal
1 pint (600 ml/2½ cups) fresh pig's blood
Salt and pepper

Chop the pork fat and onion very finely.

Put the pearl barley into a saucepan with 4 times its own volume of water and cook until soft.

Mix a little of the pig's blood with the oatmeal to make a paste, then add the cooked barley, chopped pork fat and onion, and the rest of the blood.

Season well with salt and pepper.

Spoon the mixture into a greased baking tin and bake in a moderately hot oven for 45 minutes.

If you are using intestine skin, the pudding should be boiled for 20 minutes.

Oven: 375°F/190°C Gas Mark 5

BACON AND EGG PIE

Serves 4-6

12 oz (350 g) shortcrust pastry
8 oz (225 g) bacon rashers
4 eggs
Salt and pepper

Grease an 8 inch (20 cm) flan tin.

Line with half the pastry.

Remove the rind from the bacon rashers and arrange half of them on top of the pastry.

Break in the eggs whole, and season with salt and pepper.

Arrange the rest of the bacon rashers on top.

Cover with the remaining pastry, dampening and sealing the edges.

Make two slits in the top and bake in a hot oven for 30 minutes, or until golden brown.

Oven: 425°F/220°C Gas Mark 7

PANACALTY

Serves 4

This old Yorkshire dish, cooked in a saucepan on top of the stove, used to be popular as a high tea or supper dish.

6 potatoes
1 large onion
1 lb (450 g) pork sausage or bacon
Salt and pepper

Peel and slice the potatoes lengthways.

Peel and slice the onion.

Put a little water in the bottom of a pan.

Put a layer of potato in the pan, followed by the bacon or sausages, and then the onion rings.

Add 1 pint (600 ml/2 1/2 cups) water.

Cover with a lid, bring to the boil, and simmer gently until the potatoes are cooked - this should take about 1/2 hour.

Serve hot.

OLD WIVES' SOD

Serves 4

5 eggs
3/4 pint (450 ml/2 cups) milk
Salt and pepper
1 oz (25 g) butter
2 oatcakes

Grease an ovenproof dish with butter.

Beat the eggs into a bowl, add the milk and seasoning and mix well.

Pour into the greased dish.

Break the oatcakes into small pieces and sprinkle on top.

Dot the top with butter.

Bake in a moderate oven for about 20 minutes.

Oven: 325°F/160°C   Gas Mark 3

YORKSHIRE RAREBIT

Serves 4

A tasty and nourishing dish, often known as Buck Rarebit

1 oz (25 g) butter
1 level tablespoon flour
5 tablespoons milk
6 oz (175 g) grated Wensleydale cheese
2 oz (50 g) cooked ham
1 teaspoon mixed mustard
A few drops of Worcester Sauce
Salt and pepper

Melt the butter in a saucepan and stir in the flour.

Cook for a couple of minutes, then add the milk, stirring well until it thickens.

Add the cheese, ham cut into dice, mustard and Worcester sauce. Season with salt and pepper.

Spread the mixture on to slices of butterd toast and put under a grill until golden brown.

TO MAKE CREAM CHEESE A MORE MODERN WAY

1 quart (1.15 litres/ 5 cups) fresh new milk
1 teaspoon salt

Stand the milk in a warm place for 24 hours until the curd has set.

Add the salt and stir well.

Put the curd into a cheese cloth and hang it up to drain.

When all the whey has run off turn the curd into a dish. The cheese is ready to use at once.

CHEESE

Wensleydale is the cheese of the Yorkshire Dales, and although most of it is now commercially produced, there are still a few farmers' wives in the area around Wensleydale who produce their own. The recipe for the cheese was brought to the North of England by the monks following in the wake of the Norman Conquest.

Cream cheese is also traditional in Yorkshire. Grewelthorpe, a village near Ripon in the West Riding is celebrated for the cream cheese made there. Mrs Loudon, in her *Lady's Country Companion* gives the following instructions:

'A York cream cheese is made by taking a quart of new milk warm from the cow, into which is sometimes put half a pint of cream, and adding to it two spoonfuls of the water in which a piece of rennet has steeped all night. The milk is then set before the fire till the curd is formed, when it should be taken up without breaking, if possible, and then put into a frame made of oak wood seven inches long within, four inches wide, and three inches and a half deep. This frame being open at the top and bottom, it must be placed upon rushes to permit the whey to run out; to encourage which, a board must be put within the frame to support a weight to press down the curd, between which and the curd some rushes must be put. After standing 2 days, the rushes must be renewed, when the cheese should be taken from the vat and turned as often as necessary.'

APPLE PIE

Serves 6

Apples are produced in most areas of Yorkshire. traditionally apple pie is served with Wensleydale cheese.

1 lb (450 g) cooking apples
4 oz (100 g) sugar
A pinch of cinnamon
8 oz (225 g) shortcrust pastry

Peel, core and slice the apples and arrange in a buttered pie dish.

Sprinkle over the sugar.

Add a pinch of cinnamon.

Roll out the pastry and cover the dish.

Trim and seal the edges and make a slit in the pastry.

Bake in a hot oven for 15 minutes, then reduce the temperature and bake for a further 30 minutes.

Dredge the pie with sugar and serve with Wensleydale cheese.

Oven: 425°F/220°C Gas Mark 7
Reduce to: 350°F/180°C Gas Mark 4

APPLE AND HONEY PUDDING

Serves 6

4 oz (100 g) butter
4 oz (100 g) caster sugar
2 eggs
4 oz (100 h) plain flour
A pinch of salt
2 oz (50 g) soft brown sugar
2 cooking apples
4 oz (100 g) honey
A pinch of grated nutmeg

Cream the butter and sugar together until light and fluffy.

Gradually beat in the eggs, adding a little flour to stop them curdling.

Sift the rest of the flour with the salt and fold into the mixture.

Grease a pudding basin and sprinkle the brown sugar over the bottom and round the sides.

Peel, core and slice the apples and put at the bottom of the basin with the honey and grated nutmeg.

Pour the creamed mixture over the apples.

Cover the basin with greaseproof paper, tied securely.

Steam for 1 1/2 - 2 hours, or for 45 minutes in a pressure cooker.

When cooked, turn out and serve with warmed honey or custard.

BILBERRY PLATE PIE

Serves 6-8

Bilberries used to be gathered on the bleak moors of the North and West Ridings of Yorkshire. A plate pie is one that has both a pastry base and a pastry top.

12 oz (350 g) shortcrust pastry
8 oz (225 g) bilberries (or 4 oz (100 g) bilberries and
4 oz (100 g) chopped apple
2 oz (100 g) sugar)

Roll out half the pastry to line a buttered pie plate.

Fill with the bilberries, or bilberries and chopped apple.

Sprinkle on the sugar.

Roll out the remaining pastry to make a lid.

Damp the edges of the pastry, seal and trim.

Make a slit in the top and brush with milk to glaze.

Bake in a hot oven for 15 minutes, then reduce the temperature and bake for a further 30 minutes.

Oven: 425°F/220°C Gas Mark 7
Reduce to: 350°F/180°C Gas Mark 4

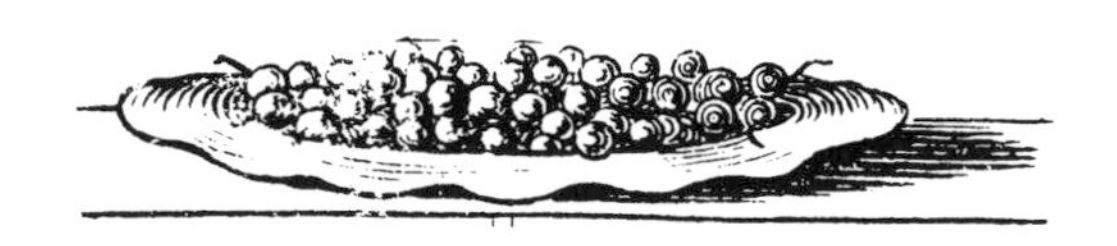

MINT PASTIES

Serves 4

8 oz (225 g) puff or shortcrust pastry
1 oz (25 g) currants
1 oz (25 g) raisins
1/2 oz (15 g) cut mixed peel
1 oz (25 g) soft brown sugar
A pinch of grated nutmeg
A sprig of freshly chopped mint - about 2 teaspoonfuls
1 oz (25 g) butter, softened

Divide the pastry into 4 equal pieces.

Roll out each piece into a round, 1/4 inch (5 mm) thick.

Mix together the currants, raisins, mixed peel, sugar, nutmeg and chopped mint.

Bind them together with the softened butter.

Divide the mixture between the 4 rounds, placing it on one half of the pastry.

Fold the other half of the pastry over the filling, dampen and seal the edges.

Place the pasties on a greased baking sheet.

Brush with milk to glaze and sprinkle with sugar.

Bake in a hot oven for 30 minutes until golden brown.

Oven: 425°F/220°C Gas Mark 7

TREACLE TART

Serves 4-6

8 oz (225 g) shortcrust pastry
4 oz (100 g) brown breadcrumbs
4 oz (100 g) mixed dried fruit
1 apple, peeled and grated
Grated rind and juice of 1 lemon
2 tablespoons treacle
1/2 teaspoon mixed spice
1/2 teaspoon ground ginger

Roll out half the pastry to line a greased flan tin or pie plate.

Mix all the filling ingredients together and spoon over the pastry base.

Roll out the remaining pastry to make a lid, dampening and sealing the edges of the tart.

Prick lightly all over and brush with milk to glaze.

Bake in a hot oven for 10 minutes , then reduce the temperature and bake for a further 20 minutes.

Oven: 425°F/220°C Gas Mark 7
Reduce to: 350°F/180°C Gas Mark 4

BAKED RICE PUDDING

Serves 4

2 oz (50 g) pudding rice
1 oz (25 g) sugar
1 oz (25 g) shredded suet
1 pint (600 ml/2$^{1/2}$ cups) milk
Grated nutmeg

Wash the rice thoroughly and put it in a buttered ovenproof dish.

Add the sugar and shredded suet, and stir in the milk.

Sprinkle the top with grated nutmeg.

Bake in a slow oven for 1$^{1/2}$-2 hours, stirring occasionally during cooking.

Oven: 300°F/150°C Gas Mark 2

WEST RIDING PUDDING

Serves 6

6 oz (175 g) shortcrust pastry
2 tablespoons raspberry jam
4 oz (100 g) butter
4 oz (100 g) caster sugar
2 eggs
4 oz (100 g) self-raising flour
1 oz (25 g) ground almonds
Grated rind of half a lemon

Line a greased pie plate with the pastry.

Spread the base with the jam.

Cream the butter and sugar together in a bowl until light and fluffy.

Beat in the eggs, one at the time, adding a little flour to stop them curdling.

Sift the flour and add to the mixture with the ground almonds and grated lemon rind.

Spoon this mixture over the jam.

Bake in a moderately hot oven for about 45 minutes, until well risen and firm.

Oven: 350°F/180°C Gas Mark 4

HASTY PUDDING

Serves 4

1 pint (600 ml/2$^{1/2}$ cups) milk
1 tablespoon oatmeal
1 tablespoon flour
Salt

Pour most of the milk into a saucepan, add the oatmeal and bring to the boil.

Mix the flour to a thin paste with the remaining milk, and add this to the boiling mixture, stirring well until it thickens.

Add a good pinch of salt.

Simmer for about 20 minutes until cooked.

Serve hot with jam.

OATCAKES

Oatcakes have for many centuries been part of the traditional Yorkshire diet. They were made in two different ways. The crisp haverbread or clapbread was rolled out from a stiff dough. The softer havercake or riddle cake was made by mixing oatmeal and buttermilk or water into a batter. This was done in a wooden kneading trough called a 'knade-kit'. Then a riddle, or backboard - a square wooden board with a handle - was sprinkled with meal and the batter was dropped on to this and 'reeled' into shape by shaking the boards with both hands. The batter was then drawn on to a piece of muslin on another board and tossed on to a backstone over an open fire.

For the haverbread:
4 oz (100 g) medium-ground oatmeal
1 oz (15 g) lard
A pinch of salt

To make the haverbread:

Melt the lard in a little hot water and add to the oatmeal and salt to form a stiff dough.

Flatten with your hand, and roll out into a large round shape.

Bake on a hot griddle until crisp.

For the havercake:
8 oz (225 g) finely-ground oatmeal
1 teaspoon bicarbonate of soda
1 pint (600 ml/2$^{1/2}$ cups) buttermilk, or milk and water

To make the havercake:

Mix the oatmeal and the bicarbonate of soda with three-quarters of the liquid - the rest may be added later as the batter begins to thicken.

Spoon a small amount of batter on to a hot greased griddle, spreading it over the whole surface with a spatula.

When the edges dry and begin to rise turn the oatcake over using a palette knife and cook the other side.

When cool the oatcakes may be buttered and spread with treacle, or eaten with cheese.

OATMEAL BISCUITS

Makes 12-15

2 oz (50 g) butter
4 oz (100 g) sugar
2 eggs
8 oz (225 g) finely-ground oatmeal
2 teaspoons baking powder

Grease two baking sheets.

Beat the butter and sugar together until light and fluffy.

Beat in the eggs, adding a little oatmeal to prevent curdling.

Add the remaining oatmeal and baking powder.

Drop tablespoonsful of the mixture on to the greased baking sheets.

Bake in a moderate oven for 15-20 minutes until golden brown.

Oven: 350°F/180°C Gas Mark 4

WAKEFIELD GINGERBREAD

Gingerbread has always been traditional in Yorkshire and, like Yorkshire pudding, every family has its own recipe. This sponge-like gingerbread is popular in the West Riding, particularly in Wakefield.

1 lb (450 g) plain flour
A pinch of salt
2 rounded teaspoons ground ginger
8 oz (225 g) sugar
5 oz (150 g) lard
8 oz (225 g) golden syrup
1 egg
1 teaspoon bicarbonate of soda
Milk to mix

Grease an 8 inch (20 cm) tin.

Sift the flour, salt and ginger into a mixing basin.

Stir in the sugar.

Melt the lard and golden syrup in a pan and stir into the dry ingredients.

Add the beaten egg.

Dissolve the bicarbonate of soda in a little milk and stir into the mixture.

Add more milk if necessary to make a thick paste.

Spread the mixture in the greased baking tin and bake in a moderate oven for 45 minutes.

Cool and cut into squares.

Oven: 350°F/180°C Gas Mark 4

CUT AND COME AGAIN CAKE

This cake is popular in the West Riding, and is traditionally eaten with Wensleydale cheese.

10 oz (275 g) self-raising flour
6 oz (175 g) butter
6 oz (175 g) soft brown sugar
12 oz (350 g) mixed dried fruit
1 oz (25 g) cut mixed peel
1/2 teaspoon cinnamon
4 eggs
1 tablespoon rum or brandy
Milk to mix

Grease and line an 8 inch (20 cm) cake tin.

Sift the flour into a mixing basin.

Cut the butter into small pieces and rub into the flour.

Add the sugar, dried fruit, mixed peel and cinnamon.

Beat the eggs.

Stir into the mixture with the rum or brandy.

Add enough milk to make a soft consistency.

Spoon the mixture into the cake tin and bake in a moderate oven for 1 1/2 hours.

Oven: 350°F/180°C Gas Mark 4

BEDALE PLUM CAKE

Plum cake got its name from the dried plums - or prunes- that traditionally were included in the recipe. This type of cake is very rich, with a high proportion of butter, sugar and eggs to the flour.

1 lb (450 g) butter
1 lb (450 g) caster sugar
9 eggs
18 oz (500 g) plain flour
2 teaspoons baking powder
2 teaspoons mixed spice
8 oz (225 g) raisins
8 oz (225 g) currants
8 oz (225 g) sultanas
4 oz (100 g) cut mixed peel
Juice and grated rind of 1 lemon

Grease and line an 9-10 inch (25 cm) cake tin.

Cream the butter and sugar until light and fluffy.

Gradually beat in the eggs, adding a little of the flour to stop them curdling.

Sift the rest of the flour with the baking powder and mixed spice, and fold into the mixture.

Add the dried fruit, mixed peel, lemon juice and grated rind.

Turn into the cake tin and level the top with a flat knife.

Bake in a moderate oven for about 2 hours, until firm and golden brown.

Oven: 350°F/180°C Gas Mark 4

YORK BUNS

Makes 12

1 lb (450 g) plain flour
1 oz (25 g) baking powder
A pinch of salt
6 oz (175 g) butter
6 oz (175 g) caster sugar
6 oz (175 g) currants
2 oz (50 g) cut mixed peel
2 eggs
About 1/2 pint (300 ml/1 1/4 cup) milk

Grease two baking sheets.

Sift the flour, baking powder and salt into a mixing basin.

Rub in the butter, cut into small pieces.

Mix in the sugar, currants and mixed peel.

Add the eggs and enough milk for a fairly stiff consistency.

Put spoonfuls of the mixture, shaped into rounds, on to the greased baking sheets.

Brush the tops with milk.

Bake in a hot oven for about 20 minutes, until golden brown.

Oven: 425°F/220°C Gas Mark 7

MOGGY

This is a very old traditional recipe. Possibly the name is derived from 'Mugi', the old Norse word for a heap of corn.

12 oz (350 g) plain flour
1 teaspoon baking powder
A pinch of salt
3 oz (75 g) lard
3 oz (75 g) margarine
4 oz (100 g) syrup
4 oz (100 g) sugar
Milk

Grease a baking sheet.

Sift the flour, baking powder and salt into a mixing basin.

Cut the lard and margarine into small pieces and rub into the flour until the mixture resembles breadcrumbs.

Stir in the syrup and sugar.

Add enough milk to make a stiff dough.

Roll out onto a floured board to a thickness of about 1 1/2 inches (3.5 cms).

Bake in a moderate oven for about 30 minutes, until nicely browned.

Cut into pieces and serve warm, spread with butter.

Oven: 350°F/180°C Gas Mark 4

FAT RASCALS

Makes 20-24

The simple scone-like cakes used to be cooked over a turf fire, or on a 'backstone'. They were also known as turf cakes.

1 lb (450 g) plain flour
A pinch of salt
8 oz (225 g) butter
4 oz (100 g) currants
4 oz (100 g) brown sugar
A little milk and water mixed

Grease two baking sheets.

Sift the flour and salt into a mixing basin.

Cut the butter into pieces and rub into the flour.

Add the currants and sugar.

Stir in enough milk and water to make a firm dough.

Roll out on a floured surface to 1/2 inch (1 cm) thick, and cut into rounds.

Place on the greased baking sheets.

Sprinkle the tops with caster sugar.

Bake in a moderately hot oven for approximately 20 minutes, until golden brown.

Oven: 375°F/190°C   Gas Mark 5

OVEN BOTTOM CAKE

These cakes used to be made from leftover bread dough. The dough was kneaded into a single large round, dimpled in the middle, and baked for 20 minutes on the bottom of a hot oven before being turned over for a further 5-10 minutes. It was then taken from the oven, torn open, thickly buttered and eaten at once.

1 1/2 lbs (675 g) plain flour
1 level teaspoon salt
1/2 oz (15 g) fresh yeast
1 level teaspoon sugar
3/4 pint (450 ml/2 cups) warm water
4 oz (100 g) lard

Sift the flour and salt into a large mixing basin.

Cream the yeast with the sugar and a little warm water and add to the flour.

Add enough water to make a smooth dough.

Knead well, cover, and leave in a warm place to rise until doubled in size.

Knock back the dough and add the lard, cut into small lumps - the cake will retain its lumpy appearance when baked.

Place on a greased baking sheet and bake in a hot oven for 15 minutes, then reduce the temperature and cook for a further 30 minutes.

Oven: 425°F/220°C Gas Mark 7
Reduce to: 375°F/190°C Gas Mark 5

TURF CAKES

Makes 12-15

These little cakes are traditionally baked on a hot griddle over a turf fire.

8 oz (225 g) self-raising flour
A pinch of salt
4 oz (100 g) lard
3 oz (75 g) sugar
3 oz (75 g) currants
1 beaten egg

Grease a baking sheet.

Sift the flour and salt into a mixing basin.

Cut the lard into small pieces and rub into the flour until the mixture resembles breadcrumbs.

Add the sugar and currants.

Stir in the beaten egg, and add a little water if necessary to make a soft dough.

Roll the dough out to the thickness of 1/2 inch (1 cm).

Cut into rounds and place them on a greased baking sheet.

Bake in a hot oven for 10-15 minutes, until the cakes are golden brown.

Oven: 425°F/220°C Gas Mark 7

RICHMOND MAIDS OF HONOUR Makes 12

The story goes that Henry VII and Anne Boleyn went for a day's hunting to Richmond, and Anne and her maids of honour were served these little tarts. Finding them delicious, Anne invited Henry to try one. He asked what they were called, and as no-one was able to tell him he named them Maids of Honour.

4 oz (100 g) puff pastry
4 oz (100 g) ground almonds
2 oz (50 g) caster sugar
1 egg
1/2 oz (15 g) flour
2 tablespoons cream
1 tablespoon orange-flower water

Grease 12 patty tins.

Roll out the pastry thinly and cut into rounds to line the greased tins.

Mix the ground almonds and sugar together.

Add the beaten egg.

Stir in the flour, cream, and orange-flower water.

Divide the mixture evenly between the 12 pastry cases.

Bake in a moderately hot oven for 25-30 minutes, until the filling is set and golden brown.

Oven: 400°F/200°C Gas Mark 6

CABLE CAKES

Makes 24

2 oz (50 g) lard
1 oz (25 g) caster sugar
8 oz (225 g) plain flour
1 level teaspoon baking powder
8 oz (225 g) mincemeat
1 egg
Milk

Grease some patty tins, or use paper cases.

Cream the lard and sugar together.

Sift the flour and baking powder together.

Add to the mixture.

Add the mincemeat.

Add the egg, and enough milk to make a stiff dough.

Spoon into the patty tins or paper cases.

Bake in a hot oven for about 15 minutes, until the cakes are golden brown and springy to the touch.

Oven: 450°F/230°C Gas Mark 8

HARROGATE SPONGE

4 eggs
4 oz (100 g) caster sugar
4 oz (100 g) plain flour
1 level teaspoon baking powder

Grease and flour two 8 inch (20 cm) sandwich tins.

Put the sugar and eggs into a bowl over simmering water and beat until thick and creamy.

Sift the flour and baking powder and fold into the mixture.

Divide the mixture equally between the two cake tins.

Bake in a moderately hot oven for about 20 minutes, until the sponge is firm and springy to the touch.

Cool on a wire rack, then sandwich the sponges together with fresh cream and jam.

Oven: 375°F/190°C   Gas Mark 5

ILKLEY CAKE

1 lb (450 g) plain flour
1 level teaspoon baking powder
1 level teaspoon salt
1 level teaspoon grated nutmeg
1 level teaspoon mixed spice
4 oz (100 g) lard
12 oz (350 g) brown sugar
8 oz (225 g) currants
4 oz (100 g) raisins
2 oz (50 g) cut mixed peel
Water to mix

Grease a 9-10 inch (25 cm) cake tin and line it with geaseproof paper.

Sift the flour, baking powder, salt and spices into a mixing basin.

Rub in the lard, cut into small pieces.

Add the sugar, dried fruit and mixed peel.

Stir in enough water to make a dropping consistency.

Spoon into the cake tin.

Bake in a moderate oven for about 2 hours, until firm and golden brown.

Oven: 350°F/180°C   Gas Mark 4

TEACAKES

Makes 12

1½ lbs (675 g) plain flour
1 level teaspoon salt
2 oz (50 g) lard
4 oz (100 g) currants
1 oz (25 g) chopped mixed peel
1 oz (25 g) fresh yeast
1 oz (25 g) sugar
12 fl oz (350 ml/1½ cups) milk and water mixed

Sift the flour and salt into a warm mixing basin.

Rub in the lard.

Add the currants and mixed peel.

Cream the yeast with the sugar.

Add them to the warmed milk.

Pour on to the flour.

Mix well to form a fairly stiff dough.

Knead lightly and leave in a warm place to rise until doubled in size.

Turn on to a floured surface and divide into 12 equal-sized pieces.

Shape into round flat cakes and put on to a greased baking sheet.

Leave to prove for a further 20 minutes.

Bake in a hot oven for about 20 minutes, or until well-risen and golden brown.

Oven: 425°F/220°C Gas Mark 7

YORK BISCUITS

Makes about 24

3 oz (75 g) butter
3 oz (75 g) caster sugar
8 oz (225 g) plain flour
1 level teaspoon baking powder
Milk to mix

Grease two baking sheets.

Cream the butter and sugar until light and fluffy.

Sift the flour and the baking powder together and fold into the creamed mixture.

Add enough milk to make a stiff dough, kneading thoroughly.

Roll out the dough on to a floured surface to a thickness of 1/8 inch (3 mm).

Cut out the biscuits with a 2 inch (5 cm) round cutter.

Place on the greased baking sheets and bake in a moderate oven for 30 minutes.

Oven: 325°F/160°C   Gas Mark 3

FRUMENTY

In the Yorkshire Dales Christmas Eve supper consisted of bowls of frumenty with pepper cake, mince pies and cheese, served by the light of the Yule candle. Frumenty was made from wheat or barley from which the husks had been removed in special 'pearling' mills.

8 oz (225 g) pearled barley or wheat
3 pints (1.75 litres) water
A pinch of salt
2 pints (1.15 litres) milk
4 oz (100 g) currants
2 oz (50 g) raisins
2 oz (50 g) sultanas
1/2 level teaspoon nutmeg
Sugar to taste
1 oz (25 g) cornflour

Put the grain into an ovenproof dish, cover with the water and add a pinch of salt.

Cook in a slow oven for several hours until the grain has 'creed' into a soft, jelly-like mass and absorbed all the water.

Add the milk, dried fruits, nutmeg and sugar to taste and put back into the oven for another 2 hours.

If necessary stir in the cornflour mixed with a little water to thicken the frumenty.

Serve the frumenty hot, with cream and rum.

Oven: 275°F/140°C Gas Mark 1

YORKSHIRE CHRISTMAS PIE

On Yorkshire estates, pies of enormous size were made at Christmas and were often sent to London as presents.

The following recipe for Yorkshire Christmas Pie appears in Hannah Glasse's '*The Art of Cookery Made Plain and Easy*' published in 1747.

'First make a good standing crust, let the wall and bottom be very thick; bone a turkey, a goose, a fowl, a partridge, and a pigeon; season them all very well, take half an ounce of mace, half an ounce of nutmeg, a quarter of an ounce of cloves, and half an ounce of black pepper, all beat fine together, two large spoonfuls of salt, and then mix them together, open the fowls all down the back, and bone them; first the pigeon, then the partridge; cover them; then the fowl, then the goose, and then the turkey, which must be large; season them all well first, and lay them in the crust, so as it will look only like a whole turkey; then have a hare ready cased and wiped with a clean cloth; cut it to pieces, then joint it; season it, and lay it as close as you can on one side; on the other side woodcocks, moor game, and what sort of wild fowl you can get; season them well and lay them close; put at least four pounds of butter into the pie, then lay on your lid, which must be a very thick one, and let it be well baked; it must have a very hot oven, and will take at least four hours.'

PEPPER CAKE

This was a traditional Christmas speciality, served on top of a large cheese, so that the two were cut together. It was offered to carol singers and other visitors, so the children used to sing:

" A little bit of pepper cake,
A little bit of cheese,
A little drink of water,
And a penny, if you please!"

12 oz (350 g) plain flour
1 teaspoon baking powder
1 oz (25 g) ground cloves
12 oz (350 g) treacle
4 oz (100 g) butter
4 oz (100 g) soft brown sugar
3 eggs

Grease and line an 8 inch (20 cm) cake tin.

Sift the flour, baking powder and cloves into a large mixing basin.

Put the treacle, butter and sugar into a saucepan and heat gently until the sugar has dissolved and the butter melted.

Pour into the flour.

Beat the eggs and add to the mixture, beating thoroughly until you have a thick paste.

Bake in a moderate oven for 1-1 1/2 hours, until the cake is firm.

Oven: 350°F/180°C Gas Mark 4

MINCEMEAT

During the Middle Ages spices and dried fruit were often cooked with meat. Until this century the 'mincemeat' in mince pies at Christmas traditionally included some minced beef or mutton. Yorkshire housewives used to make a large jar of mincemeat which they kept in a cool place in the larder. They took out the amount that was needed for a pie, then smoothed down the remainder, added a drop of brandy, and covered it up again.

This is a traditional recipe for real mincemeat, containing meat.

3 lbs (1.5 kg) boiled leg of lamb or mutton
3 lbs (1.5 kg) cooking apples
1 lb (450 g) raisins
1 lb (450 g) currants
Juice and rind of 6 lemons
1/2 teaspoon salt
Sugar to taste

Cut the boiled lamb into small pieces.

Peel, core and chop the apples.

Mince the lamb and apples together.

Add the raisins, currants, grated lemon peel and juice.

Add the salt, and enough sugar for the sweetness required.

Store in a large covered jar, in a cool place. Use as required.

RIPON SPICE BREAD

At Christmas time spice bread was offered to callers with a chunk of cheese and a glass of mulled ale.

1 lb (450 g) plain flour
A pinch of salt
2 level teaspoons mixed spice
2 oz (50 g) butter
2 oz (50 g) lard
4 oz (100 g) sugar
4 oz (100 g) currants
4 oz (100 g) raisins
1 oz (25 g) cut mixed peel
1 egg
1/2 oz (15 g) fresh yeast
A little warm milk

Sift the flour, salt and spice into a mixing basin.

Rub in the butter and lard.

Mix in the sugar, currants, raisins, mixed peel and beaten egg.

Cream the yeast with a teaspoon of sugar and a little milk.

Stir in the flour with enough milk for a firm dough.

Cover the dough and leave in a warm place to rise until doubled in size.

Knock back and put in a greased and floured 2 lb (1 kg) loaf tin.

Leave to prove for another 15 minutes, then bake in a moderately hot oven for 1 hour.

Oven: 400°F/200°C Gas Mark 6

PLUM PUDDING

A plum pudding traditionally followed the roast for Christmas Day dinner, but in the past it was much plainer than the ones we are accustomed to today. This is an 18th century recipe.

12 oz (350 g) plain flour
4 oz (100 g) butter
4 oz (100 g) sugar
4 oz (100 g) currants
4 eggs
Milk to mix

Rub the butter into the flour.

Add the sugar and currants.

Beat the eggs, and add them to the mixture with enough milk to make a stiff paste.

Pour the mixture into a floured cloth and tie securely.

Simmer in a large saucepan for 5 hours.

Serve with rum or brandy sauce.

APPLE BUTTER

Fruit butters and cheeses were made when there was a glut of fruit because a large quantity makes only a small amount of finished preserve. They are very rich and should be potted in small quantities. Small, straight-sided jars, or old cups, make suitable moulds from which preserves can be turned out whole for serving. It is best to store the butter for a year for the flavours to develop. Apple butter is traditionally served at Christmas, decorated with hazlenuts and fresh cream.

3 lbs (1.5 kg) apples - windfalls will do
1/4 pint (150 ml/2/3 cup) water or cider
1/2 teaspoon ground cloves
1/2 teaspoon cinnamon
12 oz (350 g) preserving sugar to each 1 lb (450 g) pulp

Wash the apples, put them in a pan and cover with water.

Bring to the boil and simmer until the apples are soft.

Pass the apples through a sieve, discarding the skins, core and pips.

Weigh the pulp, and allow 12 oz (350 g) sugar to each lb (450 g) fruit.

Put the fruit pulp and sugar in a pan and stir over a low heat until the sugar has dissolved.

Bring to the boil and simmer gently until the pulp is the consistency of thick cream.

Pour the apple butter into moulds and cover immediately with waxed paper discs.

When cool, put on jam covers.